### A Beginner's Guide To
# HOUSEPLANTS
#### (That Won't Kill Your Cat)

Written and Illustrated By
Kaysie Meeker

## Thank you to...

for making this knowledge necessary.
You're good cats, even though one of you ate my baby apple tree.

(Looking at you, Bandit.)

Kaysie Meeker

Houseplants (That Won't Kill Your Cat)

© 2021, Kaysie Meeker

All rights reserved.

No part of this publication may be reproduced, stored in a retrieval system, stored in a database and/or published in any form or by any means, electronic, mechanical, photocopying, recording or otherwise, without the prior written permission of the publisher.

This book is not intended as a substitute for the medical advice of trained professionals. The reader should consult a veterinarian in matters relating to the health of their pets, and particularly with respect to any symptoms that may require diagnosis or medical attention. Although the author has made every effort to ensure that the information in this book was correct at press time, the author does not assume and hereby disclaims any liability to any party for any loss, damage, or disruption caused by errors or omissions, whether such errors or omissions result from negligence, accident, or any other cause.

This book is not affiliated, associated, authorized, endorsed by, or in any way officially connected with any company, agency or government agency. All company names are trademarks™ or registered® trademarks of their respective holders. Use of them does not imply any affiliation with or endorsement by them.

# TABLE OF CONTENTS

Preface..................................................01

Air Plants............................................04
Cacti & Succulents............................05
Palms....................................................07
What's Wrong with My Houseplant?............09
Herbs....................................................11
Calathea (Prayer Plant).....................13
Ferns....................................................15
Light Zones in your Home..............17
Orchids................................................19
Peperomia..........................................21

Plant Poisoning 101........................23
List of Non-Toxic Plants................25
Glossary..............................................27
Emergency Resources...................28

Acknowledgements........................29
About the Author............................30

# PREFACE

All pet parents want to ensure that their fur-baby is safe and taken care of. One of the most critical aspects of ensuring their safety is knowing what you're bringing into your home and what could pose a risk to your cat's health.

The plants discussed in this book are certified by numerous sources to be non-toxic to your feline friend. However, it's essential to remember that being non-toxic doesn't necessarily mean that ingestion won't make your cat ill. If you notice your cat is eating your plants, they may feel stressed by something in their environment, or perhaps they're under-stimulated. Whatever the case may be, spending quality time with your cat and getting to know their behaviors and habits will allow you to identify if they are feeling ill or otherwise unwell.

Chances are, if you're reading this now, you're already a very involved pet parent who knows their baby like the back of your hand. In which case, please remember that plant poisoning is generally rare. The most at-risk felines tend to be young cats or kittens still in their curiosity stage, and the best treatment is prevention. Ensure you know what plants are in your home, and keep any unsafe plants entirely inaccessible for your pets.

With that out of the way, I'm both excited and grateful that you've taken the time to read this book. When I first became interested in houseplants, I would go to a nursery or the garden center of a local store and ask which plants were non-toxic. Typically the answer was, "I don't know," or they'd point me to one option amid the hundreds of plants available. So most of the time, I'd end up going around the store searching each plant on my phone, trying to identify for myself which ones were safe and which to avoid.

After searching numerous times for a book such as this with no results, I decided that it was time to write it myself. While making this guide, I've considered the challenges one faces when embarking upon their first indoor-gardening journey and aimed to address them in a way that is easy to follow. Most importantly, the purpose of this book is to ensure the safety of your pet. I want to give you the confidence of knowing that as you explore the hobby of indoor gardening, you can do so knowing that no harm will come to your furry, shedding, curious, nosey, erratic, crazy, lazy, moody, and ever-changing cat.

"I love cats because I enjoy my home;
and little by little,
they become its visible soul."
— Jean Cocteau

# AIR PLANTS

If your cat has a habit of knocking things over, *air plants* can be a great choice as they don't live in the soil. This also makes these plants highly portable. You'll want to keep them somewhere inaccessible to your fur baby, as there is a high chance of them picking it up and walking away with it. Remember, cats have no respect for anyone, nor any concept of personal property.

### Non-Toxic Varieties
- Cardinal Air Plant
- Red Abdita Air Plant
- Fuego Air Plant Ball
- Spanish Moss
- Peach Air Plant

## Bathe, Don't Shower

Watering air plants is the most challenging part of taking good care of them. But as a rule of thumb, water your air plant thoroughly at least once a week– more frequent watering may be needed depending on how much humidity is in the air.

The best way to water your air plant is through the soaking method. This method is pretty straightforward— fill a bowl up with water and place your air plant underwater, letting it soak for anywhere from 15 minutes to an hour. After taking it out of the water, don't forget to gently shake off any excess– this is very important to prevent root rot. It's okay if a small amount of moisture is left, as long as the plant dries out within about 4 hours.

## Location is Everything

These plants like environments that are steamy, so if possible, you should try placing them by a bathroom or kitchen window. Indirect light is best for air plants– artificial light can also be used as a light source for your air plant, as long as you ensure it is close enough to the light.

### Feline Friendly Options
- Mistletoe Cactus
- Rice Cactus
- Ric Rac Cactus
- Zebra Haworthia

## CACTI & SUCCULENTS

If you're looking for a plant as low maintenance as your cat, many cacti and other *succulents* are a perfect choice. Just like your furry friend, as long as they have a nice sunny spot to sit in, there's very little to maintain these plants.

### Do Succulents Need Water?

The short answer is yes! While cacti and *succulents* can go long periods without water, they do need it from time to time. During the winter months, your plant will go into a *dormant period* during which you won't need to water it. In the summer, only water your plant when the soil is *bone-dry*. The most common mistake you can make with these plants is overwatering, so it's often best to wait if you're ever unsure if it's time yet.

These desert-dwelling plants are very susceptible to *root rot*, so you'll want to make sure to use specially formulated high-drainage soil. Specialty soil will help to prevent excess water from lingering.

### Soak Up the Sun

Most cacti and succulents require a lot of light, so anywhere with direct lighting will be perfect for your newest additions. Windowsills are always a great choice, although you'll want to be sure to rotate your plant regularly to ensure even growth.

"Only water your [succulent] when the soil is bone-dry"

# PALMS

Palm plants are likely to be a fast favorite for both you and your fur-gremlin. While they'll love to bat at it and attempt to devour it whole, you'll surely love how low-effort and durable palms are. Like spider plants, even the most shredded palm plant can be easily mended by cutting off the affected leaf areas. It will allow for continued growth despite your cat's attempts at sabotage.

Be sure to avoid *any* palm species with the words "sago" or "cycad" in their name– they contain a high amount of the toxin *cycasin*, making them very dangerous if ingested.

> "Avoid *any* palm species with the words 'sago' or 'cycad' in their name"

(Above) *A beautiful, majestic jungle cat prepares to take a nap after a long day of other naps.*

## Water As Needed

Like cacti, the amount of water palms need is relative to the time of year it is. Palms go through a growth period in the summer, so this will be the time that it's most important to keep your palm plant on a regular watering schedule. While this hardy plant can endure drier conditions, it's best to let it slightly dry out between waterings. Regularity is best for these plants, and as you get to know your new leafy houseguest, you'll come to know its preferred schedule and location.

## Sit in the Shade

One might assume that palm plants are fans of bright light due to their association with beachy views and oceanic shorelines. However, indoor palms prefer to be kept in shadier areas. Therefore, indirect light is ideal, although your plant can even tolerate less if necessary.

### Pet–Safe Palms
*Majesty Palm, Cat Palm, Parlor Palm, Ponytail Palm*

# WHAT'S WRONG WITH MY HOUSEPLANT?

It's often easy to see when something's going wrong with your plant– their leaves may turn yellow or brown, maybe they'll even start drooping or falling off of your plant. Whatever the symptom, sick plants are distressing, and we must act quickly to keep our plants in business. Unfortunately, it is not always so simple, but thankfully there are numerous resources to help us in this age of the internet.

Typically a brief search will give you several different answers as to what your problem may be. From there, you must play detective to figure out which one applies to your situation. Some issues are relatively straightforward– if there are webs on your plant, you have *spider mites*. If the base of your money tree is going squishy, you have root rot. Others aren't so easy.

It's best to go through a little mental checklist when diagnosing your plant. First, examine your leaves closely to see if there are any signs of pests and insects. If none are visible, check the soil. Is it dried out? Or is it a little bit swampy? If neither is evident, your plant may only need more *nutrients* in its soil. You can do more research to determine what's required on a case-by-case basis, though in the meantime, I've composed a guide depicting the most common issues that you may face, as well as their solutions.

### Yellow, Wilted Leaves
*The most common cause of leaves turning yellow and wilting is overwatering. Try giving your plant more time between waterings!*

### Brown Tips
*Chemicals found in tap water can burn your leaves, causing yellow and brown tips. If you use tap water to water your plants, let it sit for 24 hours prior to watering.*

### Dry, Crunchy Leaves
*If your plant starts exhibiting these symptoms, it's likely dehydrated. Watering your plant more frequently should remedy the situation.*

### Brown Spots
*Brown spots could be a symptom of leaves being burnt by sunlight, insects/pests, or a sign of disease in the leaves. Isolate your plant and investigate further.*

### Yellow Edges
*This is a sign of either too much or too little water. Check the soil to see if it feels damp, if so give it some time to dry out. If it's dry, give your plant a thorough watering.*

### Faded, Droopy Leaves
*Faded leaves are often a sign of a plant that needs more sunlight. The best course of action is to find a new, brighter location for it.*

### Yellow Leaves That Fade To Green
*Your plant may have been sitting in wet soil for too long. Either let the soil dry out, or repot it to remove the wet soil. Let your plant dry, then modify your watering schedule.*

### Pale, Thin Leaves
*Pale leaves may mean your plant isn't receiving enough light. Try moving your plant to a location that allows it more sunlight throughout the day.*

### Torn Leaves
*Your cat is eating the plant. You can prevent this by rearranging your plants to block access to them. Hanging planters are also a great fix, as long as they're out of leaping distance.*

# HERBS

*(Above) This cat considers herself to be an Instagram influencer. She only has 437 followers, but cats can't count.*

*Herbs* are lovely because both you and your cat can eat them together. It can be a great bonding experience, and you get to escape from the hustle and bustle of daily life to pretend that you, too, are simply a chaotic feline without a care in the world.

## Soak Up the Limelight

Generally, *herbs* are pretty easy to sustain. Most herbs like a lot of sunlight, so a sunny windowsill is ideal. Make sure they're getting at least four to six hours of daylight- if the sun burns out, that's okay. You can always purchase a *grow light*. You might want to consider doing so anyways if you are thinking about growing herbs during the winter. The reduced sunlight during the winter months may slow the growth of your herbs, requiring a little extra help to keep them happy.

## Wallowing? Water.

It's recommended to water your herbs at least once a week. However, you'll be able to tell if your plant needs water sooner than that because it'll slouch and hang its little leaves down like it's moping. At which point you must give it a little bit of water and a pep talk and maybe watch a movie together or something like that.

Be careful not to overestimate how much water your herb truly needs, as it can be easy to overwater. Make sure your plant is in a pot with good *drainage*- you want your plant to remain moist without becoming waterlogged. Watch the color of your plant's leaves for signs of over and underwatering.

### Herbs To Share
*Basil, Cilantro, Sage, German Thyme\*, Dill*

\*Please note that <u>Spanish</u> *Thyme* is toxic.

## Cat-atheas

*Calathea 'Fusion White', Calathea Medallion, Calathea White Star, Peacock Plant, Pinstripe Calathea, Rattlesnake Calathea, Beauty Kim Prayer Plant, Lemon Lime Prayer Plant, Red Veined Prayer Plant*

# CALATHEA
*Prayer Plant*

Calathea receive their nickname "Prayer Plant" from the motion of their leaves through the day. During the daytime, their leaves will open up to absorb moisture, and at the end of the day, you'll see them fold vertically to retain the water they've collected. In their resting position, they look similar to a pair of praying hands. Personally, I think they're praying that they won't get eaten by your cat.

> "You'll be able to tell if your plant needs more light if the leaves struggle to unfold..."

## Let There Be Light

Calatheas are an excellent choice for beginners or the lighting-impaired due to their tolerance to different light conditions. Usually, these do best in medium to bright indirect light, but they can sometimes even tolerate lower lighting. You'll be able to tell if your plant needs more light if the leaves struggle to unfold during the day, and if your plant is receiving too much light, the leaves will begin to lose their color.

## Holy Water Not Required

Generally, prayer plants like to be watered once or twice a week, but this will vary. If you have yours in a brighter area, it may need water more often; it may require less often if it's in a dimmer area. There are no specific guidelines you need to follow. You'll figure out what works best for your plant and develop your own routine. While you're learning what works best, an excellent way to check if it's time to water is by sticking your finger in the soil a couple of inches down. If the soil beneath the surface is dry, it's probably about time to water.

# FERNS

Ferns have been known to be a bit difficult while you're getting to know them, though I've found that once you get familiar with each other, they're a rewarding plant to keep! You can brighten any room with a fern. Their voluptuous leaves and deep green color are not only beautiful, but they also have benefits. Unlike your cat, ferns are kind enough to clean your home's air in exchange for your care.

## Check Your Lighting

As with any plant, it is important to ensure your fern is given the correct amount of light. Ferns can be sensitive, and too much direct light will cause the ends of their leaves to turn brown and brittle. However if you leave them in too dark a corner, they will not get enough light to thrive. The best habitat for your indoor fern would be somewhere with indirect light where its leaves will not burn due to the harsh sun.

## Humid Air = Great Care

Ferns are big fans of humidity, so it's essential to consider this when caring for your fern. There are many ways to trick your plant into thinking your house is a nice little bog just like the one its ancestors came from, thus enabling your fern to thrive.

To trick your fern into growing, make sure you don't let it dry out. Watering 2-3 times a week is recommended, but this varies based on how much sunlight it gets, among other factors such as the mood of your fern.

A good trick for any humidity-loving plant is placing them in a bathroom or kitchen. These rooms are naturally very humid, and that can work to our advantage. You could also place the pot on top of a small tray of pebbles and water. It's important to make sure the bottom of the pot is not in the water but instead on top of the stones. If the plant's butt is in the water, it'll get root rot, and that's just a bad time for everyone involved.

## Feline-Friendly Ferns

- *Bird's Nest Fern*
- *Sharktooth Fern*
- *Bold Sword Fern*
- *Silver Lace Fern*
- *Boston Fern*
- *Staghorn Fern*
- *Maidenhair Fern*

South-facing windows receive the most light throughout the day. Keep this in mind when finding a home for your cacti, succulents, and any other plants that enjoy a lot of sunlight!

## Orchids Are Okay
*Most orchids are non-toxic if ingested. Although it is always a good idea to verify with your vet, or call the ASPCA® Poison Control Hotline (pg. 28) if you're unsure.*

# ORCHIDS

Despite being the horticultural free-loaders of the plant world, orchids are beautiful and long-lasting plants that won't kill your beloved cat. It's been said that orchids can live for nearly a century– I mean, let's be honest with ourselves, it won't live for a century, but it _could_.

If your orchid begins to drop flowers, don't be alarmed! Dropping flowers is normal and is followed by a period of new growth and fresh blooms. Don't give up on your little guy just yet.

## Take a Dip

Generally, you'll want to water your orchid every one to two weeks, depending on how dry the soil has become and what kind of lighting your orchid is in. As opposed to traditional watering, orchids respond well to a method called "_bottom-watering._"

This method involves filling a bowl full of water and setting the pot inside the bowl. The plant will pull water through the drainage hole towards the roots, ensuring the roots are thoroughly hydrated. Usually, around 10-20 minutes in the water should be sufficient.

## Lots of Light

Pay attention to the leaves of your orchid, as they will have a lot to say about its well-being. Orchids thrive on bright, indirect light. An orchid that's not receiving enough light will have dark green leaves, while a plant that's getting too much light will have leaves that have turned yellowish-green and sometimes even red. Try to keep your orchid near a window facing the south or the east to have the most success. The sunlight coming from these directions should be ideal.

# PEPEROMIA

If you're ever unsure of what plant to get, any variety of *peperomia* is a great way to go. The entire peperomia family is considered non-toxic, so there's no way you can go wrong. Not only are they non-toxic to your cats, but they're non-toxic to you as well. ~~So if you're tempted, go ahead, take a bite. I can almost guarantee you'll hate it, but feel free to try it anyway.~~ Actually, no, scratch that. Do not eat your plants.*

*(Above) This ratchety old white cat has been calloused by the feral life. Who can he trust? Nobody. Only his friend, the snail.*

## Light On Space

Most species of peperomia prefer to live in bright, indirect lighting. That's the case for many plants, so you may have to get a little bit creative to keep from running out of plant space. Sure, for now, it's just one plant– which will soon turn into 2, 3, 5, and before you know it, you don't know where the plants end and your home begins.

"The entire peperomia family is considered non-toxic..."

### Popular Peperomias
- Chinese Money Plant
- String of Turtles
- Teardrop Peperomia
- Trailing Jade Peperomia
- Cupid Peperomia
- Watermelon Peperomia

*I am absolutely not responsible for whatever happens if you decide to eat your houseplants. Unless it's super cool, then I might take a little credit.

## Wait To Water

You must be careful not to overwater your peperomia because it will get angry and die. Instead, wait until the soil has gotten relatively dry before you water it to prevent root rot. It's also a good idea to make sure the pot you keep it in has good drainage, so be careful about purchasing pots online if you don't know whether they have drainage holes. Another handy trick to keep water moving through the plant rather than settling in is to use orchid potting mix. Orchid potting mix is composed of large wood chips, among other elements, which keep air moving through the soil.

# PLANT POISONING 101

## Avoid Consumption

The most important thing you can do to protect your furry housemate is to keep yourself informed. Know the names of the plants in your house, and verify that they are safe to have around. If you happen to have toxic plants, you must keep them out of reach of your pets. Whether that's by keeping them in a room your cat is not allowed to access or by hanging them in a spot that you have confirmed to be out of their reach, do whatever you can to keep them away from your overly curious feline.

## Respond Quickly

As with any other pet-related incident or emergency, your first step should be to remove the danger to your cat and contact your vet immediately. If your vet's office is closed, you should call the ASPCA® poison control center (see page 28).

To prevent further ingestion, you'll want to wipe off any plant matter left on their mouth, fur, or paws. You can do this with a damp towel with a minimal amount of non-irritating dish soap on it. Next, take note of what plant they've gotten into so that your vet will have an easier time identifying what toxic component is causing your cat's reaction. If possible, bring a sample for the vet to examine— this could be a piece of the leaf or even a sample of vomit if present.

## Identify the Signs

Cats are notorious explorers, and if your cat happens to get into a toxic plant, you must be able to identify the signs of plant poisoning. Keep an eye out for the following symptoms.

### Irritation
- Red, watery eyes
- Itchy, scratchy
- Swelling
- Irritation around the mouth

### Gastrointestinal Symptoms
- Vomiting
- Diarrhea

### Other Serious Symptoms
- Dilated pupils
- Breathing difficulties, panting
- Irregular or rapid heartbeat
- Drooling, difficulties swallowing
- Excessive drinking and urination

# EMERGENCY RESOURCES

_____

Primary Veterinary Clinic

_____

Emergency Phone Number

In case of emergency, contact the ASPCA® Animal Poison Control Center.
Available 24 hours a day, 365 days a year.
(888) 426-4435 | aspca.org

# ACKNOWLEDGEMENTS

Thank you to my parents, Danny and Kendra Meeker, for believing in me so hard that I have no choice but to believe in myself too.

Thank you to my grandma Mommo for sending me countless articles about both cats and plants at 3 o'clock in the morning. A very late thank you to my grandpa, Poppo, who was teaching me about taking care of plants even way back when I didn't actually want to know about it. I miss you more than I thought I could, and I'll always pull the dead heads off of petunias, just like you taught me.

Thank you to my grandma, Mima, for always having a gorgeous garden that made me long for one of my own. And of course, thank you to my grandpa, Papa, for being quietly proud of me in everything I do. Nothing makes me happier than your gently spoken words of encouragement when I show you my work.

Thank you to my sisters, Brooklyn and Baylie, for being my best friends for my whole entire life. And thank you to my brother Matt for teaching me that home is wherever you make it.

Thank you to my anxiety for making me accumulate this information out of fear. Thank you also to my new friend Jessica Cheney for the time you've spent editing this book for me. You really went above and beyond, and I appreciate you greatly.

Thank you to Watson, the first cat I've ever loved as my own. You've been by my side every time I've sat down to work on this book- you're my little buddy, and you'll always hold a special place in my heart.

Finally, thank you to my beloved Shelby for being everything I've ever wanted and needed in a partner. Your support, love, pride, and encouragement helped me push through even when I thought no one would ever read this.

# ABOUT THE AUTHOR

Kaysie Meeker was born and raised just outside of Kansas City by her plant-killing mother and a firefighter father who prefers burning fields over pulling weeds. Growing up Kaysie enjoyed spending time with her two sisters, as well as their cats Saber and Smidgen. In 2019, Kaysie graduated from the University of Kansas with a Bachelor's in Graphic Design, along with a minor in Fine Arts. Shortly after graduating she brought home her very first house plant, which she swore was going to be her only one. (It wasn't)

Watson is a crazy red Abyssinian who loves attention, kisses, running at the speed of light, and finding his way to the very highest spots he can reach. Watson can often be found on top of the refrid6gerator, and is known to spend a significant amount of time sitting on the shoulders of his humans. He loves quiet time, as well as sniffing plastic grocery bags and scaring any bird who dares to perch outside his window. Watson was born in late 2015, and has been causing chaos ever since.

Photos generously provided by the following talented creators via Unsplash®

Janko Ferlic, Hannah Busing, Ian Keefe, Jason Leung, Max 3, Pelayo Arbues,
Dorien Monnens, Sanjan Shetty, Chris Abney, Matt Seymour,
Alexander Schimmeck, Jay Jay, Olena Sergienko, Paulina H., Caleb Woods,
Magali Merzougui, Olena Shmahalo, Severin Candrian, Ardi Evans,
Ignat Kushanrev, Luisa Brimble, Alvan Nee, Minh Tri, The Creative Exchange,
Timo C. Dinger, Salome Guruli, Marifer, Ergita Sela, Leonie Zettl

Made in the USA
Coppell, TX
08 February 2023